PUELLA MAGI MADOKA★MAGICA ~The different story~ 1

ART
HANOKAGE

ORIGINAL STORY
MAGICA QUARTET

~The different story~

PUELLA MAGI MADOKA MAGICA

1

EPISODE

PAGE

BU
(VOOM)
BU
BU
DO
(BLAM)

CHA (CLICK)
DO (BLAM)
HYAAAH!
GAKIN (CLANG)
HM?
PARI (VZZT)
HYU (FOOM)
BIRIRI (BZZT)

BACHII (VACCHHT)
OWWW...!
THIS ISN'T GOING TO WORK! LET'S GET OUT OF HERE!
YOU, MAGICAL GIRL OVER THERE!
SORRY! WE KNOW YOU CAME TO HELP US, BUT...
...WE'RE GOING TO HAVE TO RETREAT...!
EH!?

IF THINGS GET TOO ROUGH FOR YOU, I SUGGEST YOU RUN TOO!
BUT...
AAH!!
BASHI (VASSH)

OH, NO...!

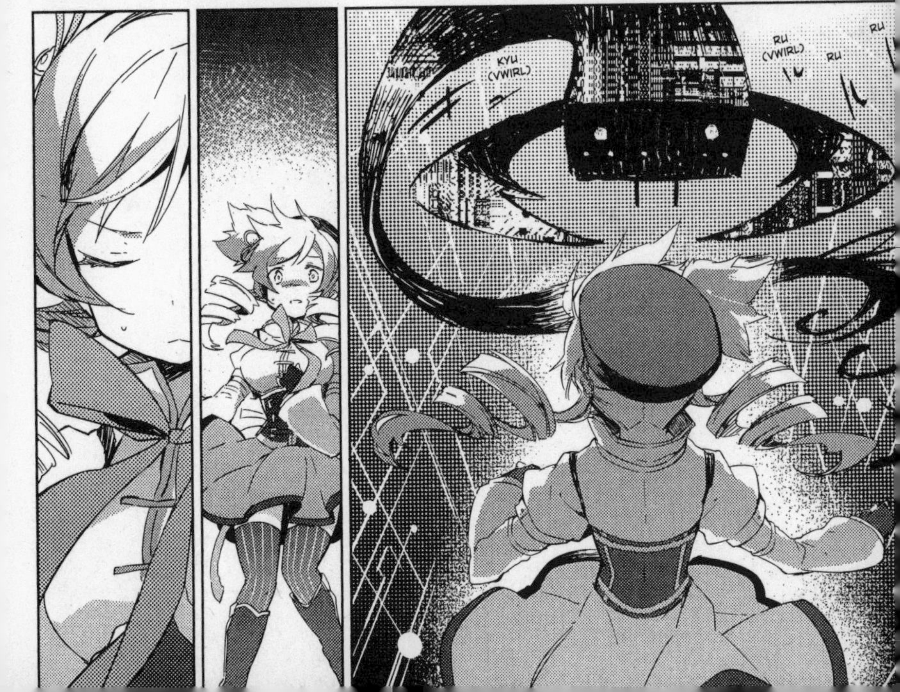
RU
RU (VWIRL)
RU
KYU (VWIRL)

GOOO (RUMMBLE)
KYURU
GYWA (ZLUWAA)

GO (GROHH)
SU (SST)
WE'RE DOING THIS TO PROTECT THE PEOPLE OF THIS TOWN...
JAKI (KACHAK)
THERE'S NO WAY I CAN...
...RUN AWAY FROM HERE...!

JIRI (VZZT)
PAAN (VWAAN)
KIIN (KEEND)
THAT...WAS AMAZING!
YOU TOOK DOWN THAT WITCH ALL ALONE!

WE'RE SORRY FOR RUNNING AWAY...
...BUT WE DIDN'T WANT TO DIE THERE.
Y-YES... WELL, I'M HAPPY THAT YOU BOTH ARE SAFE.
AND YOU USED UP YOUR MAGIC FIGHTING THE WITCH.
SO THIS TIME, I SUPPOSE IT'S FOR THE BEST.
SO...
...PERHAPS YOU TWO SHOULD USE THIS AS WELL.
WE ALL COMBINED TO DEFEAT THE WITCH.
YOU'RE NEW, AREN'T YOU?
? YES...

A BIT OF ADVICE— DON'T DO THAT.
THAT'S SOMETHING THAT YOU EARNED. YOU GOT NO REASON TO LET ANYBODY ELSE TOUCH IT.
RIGHT, RIGHT.
YOU RISKED YOUR LIFE TO GET YOUR HANDS ON IT. TREAT IT LIKE A TREASURE.
AFTER ALL, WE AREN'T FIGHTING THESE WITCHES JUST FOR THE SAKE OF "GOOD."
YOU CAN CONSIDER ALL OTHER MAGICAL GIRLS AS SOMETHING LIKE RIVALS.
I-IS THAT RIGHT ...?
IF YOU GO TREATING EVERYBODY SO NICELY...
...THEN YOU'LL END UP GETTING USED AND HAVING THE RUG PULLED OUT FROM UNDER YOU.

SO...TAKE CARE OF YOURSELF, OKAY?
DON'T OVERDO IT. YOU ONLY HAVE ONE LIFE, SO PROTECT IT.

NEXT TIME, WE'RE GONNA GET THAT GRIEF SEED!
DON'T GO MISTAKING A FAMILIAR FOR A WITCH ANYMORE, OKAY?
AH HA HA!
...... AH...

PUELLA MAGI
MADOKA MAGICA
~The different story~
EPISODE 1

ONE YEAR LATER...
TOMOE-SAAAN!
WE ALL DECIDED TO GO TO THE MALL TODAY TO DO SOME SHOPPING.
HOW ABOUT YOU?
WHY NOT COME WITH US ONCE IN A WHILE?
HMM... SORRY. I HAVE ERRANDS.
MMM...
IT MUST BE A LOT OF EXTRA WORK LIVING ON YOUR OWN, HUH?

I WANT TO GO TO YOUR PLACE AGAIN SOON! THAT CAKE YOU HAD WAS SO DELICIOUS!
WE'RE HEADED OUT!
THERE YOU GO AGAIN...
SORRY! THANKS FOR INVITING ME!
HEH-HEH...
THANK YOU!
SU (SST)
PAA (VWAA)
...... A MAGICAL GIRL...
... NOW...

TIME TO GET TO WORK!
IT'S A NAME FOR GIRLS WHO TAKE ON THE HEAVY DESTINY...

...OF FIGHTING AGAINST A CURSE THAT PLAGUES THE WORLD...
...IN EXCHANGE FOR JUST ONE SINGLE MIRACLE.

KIIIN (KEEEN)
AND SO, TODAY TOO, WITHOUT THE WORLD REALIZING IT...
...I WILL FIGHT ANOTHER WITCH.

JI (ZHEET) JI
THE WARD IS A BIT WARPED.
IS SOMEONE ALREADY IN THERE?
KIN (CLANG)
GA (WHAM)
GIIIN (CLANK)
KH!
YOU GOT MORE POWER THAN YOU KNOW WHAT TO DO WITH! JUST LIKE LAST TIME!
ZAZAZA (SKRRRRCH)

GOO (VWOOH)
CHA (SHING)
BUT THIS TIME...
...IT WON'T GO LIKE IT DID BEFORE!
DA (DASH)
TO (TUMP)
CHAKI (CHANG)

BUO (VWOH)
TA (TMP)
SORRY, BUT THAT ONE...
ZAHYU (ZWASH)
...WAS THE FAKE!

TA
(TUMP)
GARAN
(KALANG)
... GOT IT!
I FINALLY GOT MY REVENGE, HUH...
...KYUBEY?
HYU
(FOOM)
!
NOT YET...
KOOOOOO
(HYOOOHHH)
... KYOUKO.

DO (BLAM)
DO
KASHAN (CRASH)
GOU (VWHOOM)
WHOA ...!?
GYURURU (VWIRL)

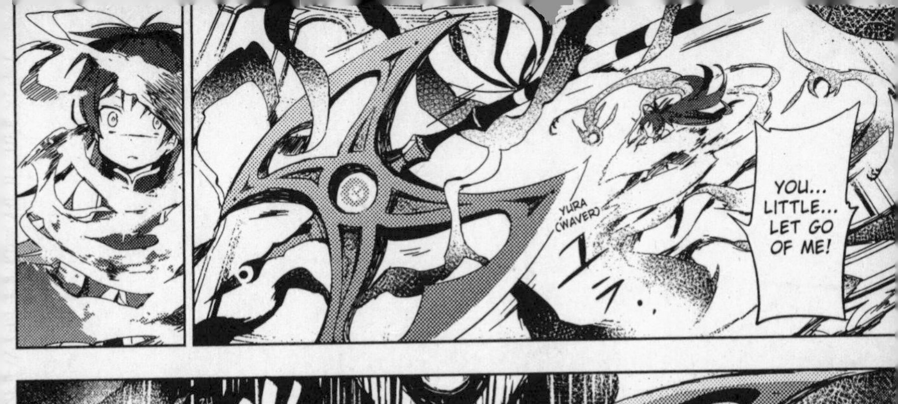
YOU... LITTLE... LET GO OF ME!
YURA (WAVER)

ZU
ZU
ZU (DOOM)
AH...
—NOT GOOD...
IF I DON'T DO SOME-THING TO STOP IT...

...I'M GONNA...
—!!
KYURURU (VWIRL)
PASHIN (SHAKK)
?
KOTSUN (TAK)
...I SEE. YOU USE FASCINATION MAGIC. INTERESTING POWER.
HOW-EVER...

!?
...SINCE THE WITCH HAS THE SAME ABILITY, I'D SAY THAT'S BAD LUCK FOR YOU.
TO (TUMP)
A MAGICAL GIRL?
GYUN (WHOOM)

DON
(BLAM)
TIRO FINALE!
GOO
(GWOOGH)
HYU
(FOOM)
WHOA!
TOSUN
(THUMP)
I'M GLAD I MADE IT IN TIME.

ARE YOU ALL RIGHT?
...YEAH, UM... THANKS FOR SAVING ME.
WHO'RE YOU...?
WE'LL SAVE INTRO-DUCTIONS FOR AFTER. RIGHT NOW, WE HAVE TO FINISH OFF THE WITCH.
I SUSPECT THE HEART OF THAT WITCH IS IN ITS AXE.
GUI (MISSING)
GUI
EH?
THAT'S HOW IT COULD COME BACK TO LIFE AFTER WE THOUGHT WE DESTROYED ITS BODY.

I'LL TAKE CARE OF THE WITCH'S BODY AND THE FAMILIARS.
WHILE I'M DOING THAT, COULD YOU DESTROY ITS HEART?
......

PARA (SCATTER)
GOT IT!

HYU
(FOOM)
GA
GA
PASHI
(GRAB)
GA
(CRUNCH)
GA
KA
GA
SU
(SST)
KASHI
(KACHIK)
DO
(BLAM)
DO
DO
DO
DO

DON
FUOON
(FWOOM)
GOO
(GWOOGH)
NOW!

HYAAAHH!
KA (KAKK)
PAKIIIIN (CRAKOOM)
PISHI (CRACK)

W......
WE DID IT!
EXCELLENT WORK.
GOO (SHOOM)

...NOW, SHALL WE INTRODUCE OURSELVES?
I AM MAMI TOMOE.
A MAGICAL GIRL FROM MITAKIHARA CITY.
AND YOU?
I'M KYOUKO SAKURA.
I'M DOING MAGICAL GIRL STUFF IN THE NEXT TOWN OVER, KAZAMINO.
YOU REALLY HELPED ME OUT BACK THERE!
IF YOU HADN'T BEEN HERE, I'D HAVE GONE DOWN FOR SURE.
IT WAS MY PLEA-SURE.
BY THE WAY, SAKURA-SAN, WHAT BRINGS YOU TO MITAKIHARA?
UM...

I'VE BEEN CHASING THAT WITCH.
THAT WITCH WAS THE FIRST ONE I FOUGHT WHEN I BECAME A MAGICAL GIRL.
BUT I LET MY GUARD DOWN JUST ONCE, AND IT GOT AWAY.
I KNOW IT'S AGAINST THE UNWRITTEN RULES TO GO INTO SOMEBODY ELSE'S TERRITORY...
...BUT I WAS WILLING TO DO ANYTHING TO BE THE ONE TO TAKE THAT WITCH DOWN.
......I SEE...

IN THE END, I WOUND UP STEPPING ON YOUR TOES, HUH?
I DON'T MIND.
THE MOST IMPORTANT THING IS THAT WE SAVE AS MANY CIVILIANS AS POSSIBLE.
AND I DON'T THINK MAGICAL GIRLS SHOULD BE FIGHTING OVER TERRITORY.

...OKAY, THEN! I TOOK OUT THE WITCH I WANTED TO.
SO I'LL JUST...
WAIT!
YOU'VE USED SOME OF YOUR MAGIC, RIGHT?
YOU HAVE TO DRAW OUT THE IMPURITIES FROM YOUR SOUL GEM.
?
BUT I DON'T REALLY HAVE THE RIGHT TO TAKE THAT TODAY.
WE BOTH TOOK IT DOWN. THIS IS THE RESULT.
ARE YOU SURE?

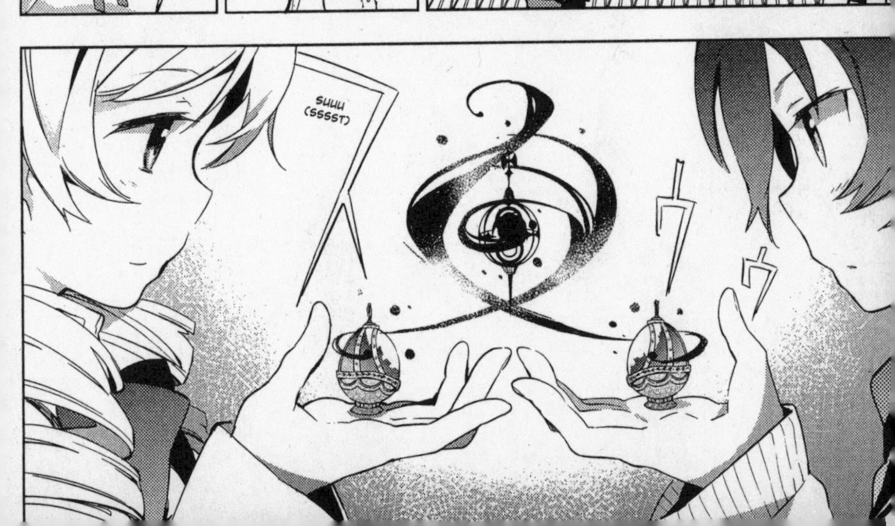
SUUU (SSSST)

EH-HEH-HEH... THANKS.
I'LL DISPOSE OF THE USED GRIEF SEED.
SAY, SAKURA-SAN?
I'M WONDERING IF YOU HAVE A LITTLE FREE TIME RIGHT NOW?
I'M NOT IN A HURRY, BUT...
?
WHAT'S UP?
PLEASE, BE MY GUEST. HAVE SOME.
ぱあぁ
PAAAA (GLOW)

THIS IS SO GOOD!
IT'S MY SPECIALTY, PEACH PIE.
I'M SORRY TO KEEP YOU WAITING SO LONG WHILE IT BAKED.
THERE'S QUITE A LOT, SO HAVE AS MUCH AS YOU LIKE.
I CERTAINLY COULD NOT EAT IT ALL BY MYSELF.
SFX: NIKO (SMILE) NIKO
AH... UM...
YOU SAVE MY BUTT, AND THEN YOU TREAT ME TO PIE.
I GOT SOME NERVE ACCEPTING IT ALL, DON'T I?
I'M THE ONE WHO INVITED YOU, SO DON'T WORRY.
IT'S A LOT OF FUN TO HAVE TEA WITH ANOTHER MAGICAL GIRL.
SURE, IF YOU SAY SO...
BUT THAT GOES DOUBLE FOR ME.
MAN, IT WAS GOOD TO MEET YOU TODAY!

I'M STILL A ROOKIE AS A MAGICAL GIRL.
IT'S A REAL LEARNING EXPERIENCE TALKING TO YOU AND DRINKING TEA.
HERE I AM JUST FIGHTING WHICHEVER WAY POPS INTO MY HEAD, BUT ON THE OTHER HAND...
...YOU'RE TAKING ALL THESE NOTES ANALYZING ALL THE WITCHES YOU'VE FOUGHT.
AND YOU'RE ALSO DOING RESEARCH ON HOW TO USE MAGIC.
AND ON TOP OF THAT, YOU'RE FULLY MENTALLY PREPARED TO FIGHT WITCHES.

IT'S NOT JUST ALL THEORY, YOU WERE REALLY STRONG IN THE ACTUAL BATTLE AS WELL.

I GOTTA SAY I'M SURPRISED THERE'S SUCH AN ACCOMPLISHED MAGICAL GIRL JUST THE NEXT TOWN OVER.

SO WHAT I'M SAYING IS... UM...
?
MAMI-SAN...
IF IT'S NOT TOO MUCH TO ASK.

...WOULD YOU MIND...

...MAKING ME YOUR DISCIPLE!?

KYOUKO OF THE PAST.
IT'S A BIT MORE MATURE
THAN THE FLASHBACKS
SHE HAD IN THE ANIME.

PUELLA MAGI

MADOKA★MAGICA

~The different story~

OH, COME ON, TOMOE-SAN!
YOU'VE BEEN IN A HAPPY DAZE ALL DAY!
DID SOMETHING GOOD HAPPEN TO YOU?
EPISODE 2
YOU WERE EVEN SPACEY DURING CLASS.
...W-WAS I REALLY?
SO THE QUESTION IS...
...YOU GOT YOURSELF A BOYFRIEND?
HUH?

WHAT'S THIS? TOMOE-SAN HAS A BOY-FRIEND?
SUSPI-CIOUS!
N-NO, I DON'T!
UM...
I DID MAKE...A FRIEND...
WHAT'S THAT MEAN?
THAT WE'RE NOT YOUR FRIENDS...?
EH!?
NO, THAT ISN'T WHAT I MEANT!
...I DON'T KNOW HOW TO SAY IT...
IT'S A LITTLE DIFFERENT FROM MY NORMAL FRIENDS.
IN A WAY...
...IF WE DIDN'T TRUST EACH OTHER BEYOND BEING JUST FRIENDS...
...THEN I DON'T THINK WE COULD BE AS COMPATIBLE.

WE'VE ONLY JUST MET, SO I CAN'T SAY FOR SURE THAT IT WILL TURN OUT THAT WAY.
...BUT I'M HOPING SHE CAN BECOME SOMEONE I CAN FEEL AT EASE ENTRUSTING MY LIFE TO...
?
...OKAY, NOT A BOYFRIEND. A FIANCÉ.
EHH?
A MAGICAL GIRL LIKE ME...
...MADE A MAGICAL GIRL FRIEND.
M... MY DISCIPLE?
RIGHT!

MAMI-SAN, YOU'RE MY IDEAL IN EVERY WAY.
SO IF I'M NOT IN YOUR WAY...
IS THE ANSWER "NO"?
......UM...
IT ISN'T QUITE THE SAME THING AS A DISCIPLE, BUT...
...FOR A LONG TIME, I'VE THOUGHT...
...THAT IT'D BE NICE TO HAVE A MAGICAL GIRL FOR A FRIEND.
SO YOU'RE SAYING...
AND THAT'S THE TRUTH.
YES.

IF I HAVE ANY ADVICE TO GIVE...
...I DON'T MIND ADVISING YOU AS A MORE EXPERIENCED "SENPAI" MAGICAL GIRL.
THANK YOU, MAMI-SAN!

THAT'S IT FOR ME FOR TODAY. THANKS FOR TREATING ME TO DINNER AGAIN!
YES, BE CAREFUL ON YOUR WAY HOME.
SAKURA-SAN...
BE SURE TO COME BY MITAKIHARA AGAIN! YOU'RE ALWAYS WELCOME!
I'M NOT IN THE WAY?
YOU'RE A HUGE HELP!
EVEN IN TODAY'S FIGHT, I COULD REALLY RELY ON YOU.
IS THAT SO...!?
RIGHT! THE SAME GOES FOR ME TOO!
LET'S SPEND A LOT OF TIME TOGETHER, OKAY?
MAMI-SENPAI!

SE...
SENPAI...?
IS THAT WHAT I AM?
I SUPPOSE SO. BUT IT'S THE FIRST TIME I'VE EVER BEEN A SENPAI.
I'M A LITTLE EMBARRASSED.
EVER SINCE I BECAME A MAGICAL GIRL...
...ALL I'VE EVER DONE IS FIGHT WITCHES EVERY DAY.
IT ISN'T LIKE THAT LEAVES ME TIME TO BE IN A SCHOOL CLUB.
...YES. THIS MIGHT NOT BE TOO BAD.
WHAT DO YOU THINK WOULD BE THE BEST NAME TO GIVE THAT GIRL'S FINAL ATTACK?
THAT ISN'T MY AREA OF EXPERTISE.

I STILL CAN'T GET OVER HOW ACCURATE YOUR WITCH-FINDING IS, MAMI-SAN!
I WAS NEVER ABLE TO FIND WITCHES THAT FAST WHEN I WAS WORKING ALONE.
THERE ARE A LOT OF UNEXPLAINED SUICIDES AND MURDERS THAT YOU CAN ATTRIBUTE TO A WITCH.
OR TO PUT IT THE OPPOSITE WAY...
...I THINK WITCHES ARE ATTRACTED TO PLACES WHERE HUMANS ARE IN DESPAIR.
WHEN YOU FIND A PLACE THAT'S A CROSSROAD FOR TROUBLED HEARTS, THEN THERE SHOULD BE SOME KIND OF DARKNESS NEARBY.
SO I START MY SEARCHES AROUND THE CENTERS OF THOSE PLACES.

I THINK IT'S VERY IMPORTANT TO FIND WITCHES AS QUICKLY AS POSSIBLE...
...TO LIMIT THE DAMAGE AND EFFECT ON HUMAN SOCIETY.
.....
SAY, MAMI-SAN...
...ABOUT HOW YOUNG WERE YOU WHEN YOU BECAME A MAGICAL GIRL?
WHY DO YOU ASK?
I'M JUST CURIOUS...
SHIRURU (SLOOOM)
TO BECOME AN ACCOMPLISHED MAGICAL GIRL WITH ALL OF YOUR ATTACKS AND KNOWLEDGE...
...I'M THINKING MAYBE IT TOOK A LONG TIME AND A LOT OF EFFORT.
ALSO...
...IT MAKES ME WONDER WHAT KIND OF WISH STARTED YOU OFF IN THE FIRST PLACE.
OH...!
I SAID SOMETHING BAD, DIDN'T I?
NO...
I SUPPOSE NOW IS A GOOD TIME.
I'VE BEEN MEANING TO TELL YOU...

I MADE MY CONTRACT ABOUT A YEAR AGO.
(POIT)
IF I HADN'T MET KYUBEY... I WOULDN'T BE A PART OF THE WORLD RIGHT NOW.
MY CONTRACT WITH THIS GUY KEPT ME ALIVE.
A YEAR AGO, MY FAMILY AND I WERE IN A TERRIBLE ACCIDENT...
AND BECAUSE OF THE QUICK CONTRACT, I WAS THE ONLY SURVIVOR.
IT TURNED OUT THAT MY PARENTS DIDN'T MAKE IT.
IT WAS VERY PAINFUL AND SAD.
BUT WITH A FATE TO BATTLE WITCHES, I COULDN'T MOURN FOREVER.
AT ONE POINT, I STARTED TO THINK...

...IF SOMEONE IS KILLED BY A WITCH OR FAMILIAR, I'M SURE SOMEONE ELSE WILL FEEL THE SAME SORROW I DID.
AND AS A RESULT OF MY LIFE BEING SAVED, I RECEIVED THE POWER TO FIGHT WITCHES.
IF, THROUGH MY EFFORTS FIGHTING WITCHES, EVEN ONE PERSON IS SPARED MY SORROW, IT'S WORTH IT.
SO I THOUGHT... IT WAS BEST FOR ME TO KEEP FIGHTING.
IT'S THAT THOUGHT...
...THAT PROBABLY KEEPS ME DOING WHAT I'M DOING NOW.
AND THAT'S WHY I'M SO HAPPY THAT YOU'RE FIGHTING WITH ME, SAKURA-SAN.
...I SEE.
YOU'RE THE VERY FIRST PERSON WHO EVER RECOGNIZED MY WAY OF FIGHTING.
....

NOW, LET'S CALL IT A DAY AND GO BACK TO HAVE SOME TEA.
HEY, LISTEN...

HOW ABOUT INSTEAD OF GOING TO YOUR PLACE...
...IF IT'S OKAY WITH YOU WITH YOU...WOULD YOU COME TO MY HOUSE?

BIG SISTER MAMI-CHAAAN!
PAA (SHINE)

PLAY WITH ME! PLAY WITH ME!
WE ONLY JUST FINISHED DINNER, SO LEAVE IT FOR LATER.
STOP THAT, MOMO!
AWW!

PLEASE FORGIVE US. MY YOUNGEST ALWAYS GETS SO EXCITED WHENEVER WE HAVE GUESTS.
THEN YOU PLAY WITH ME, DADDY!
ME?
IT'S SO ENERGETIC HERE, I'M HAVING A LOT OF FUN!
HONESTLY... IF YOU HAD JUST TOLD ME BEFORE-HAND...
...I COULD HAVE MADE SOMETHING MORE APPRO-PRIATE!
THANK YOU SO MUCH...
...FOR THE LOVELY DINNER!
IT'S BETTER TO HAVE WHAT WE ALWAYS HAVE!
IF IT WAS TOO GOOD, MAMI-SAN WOULD FEEL GUILTY ABOUT COMING OVER.

IT'S BEEN SO LONG SINCE I'VE HAD SUCH A HAPPY DINNER.
I REALLY APPRECIATE IT.
WE'RE HAPPY THAT YOU ENJOYED IT.
TO BE PERFECTLY HONEST, NOW WE CAN TREAT OUR GUESTS TO A MEAL THAT DOESN'T EMBARRASS US, BUT...
...THAT'S ONLY A RECENT DEVELOPMENT.
IS THAT SO?
IT IS.
I SERVE AS PASTOR TO MY CHURCH'S FLOCK.
MY SERMONS ARE MEANT TO BRING A BIT MORE HAPPINESS TO THE WORLD.
HOWEVER, FOR YEARS, NO ONE WOULD LEND AN EAR TO THEM.
AND MY FAMILY SUFFERED BECAUSE OF IT.
THEN, IT ALL CHANGED FROM ONE DAY TO THE NEXT...
...AND FOLLOWERS WHO WISHED TO HEAR MY MESSAGE STARTED APPEARING.

INDEED, I DOUBTED THE EVIDENCE OF MY OWN EYES.
ONE MORNING, AS I AWOKE, THERE WAS A LARGE NUMBER OF PEOPLE THERE...
...AND THEY HAD ALL GATHERED TO HEAR MY SERMON.
IF YOU BELIEVE AND CONTINUE TO PLANT THE SEEDS OF THAT FAITH...
...THEN THOSE SEEDS MAY FINALLY FLOWER.
THAT IS SOMETHING MY HUSBAND ONCE SAID.

...I SEE.

AFTER ALL, YOU'RE THE FIRST FRIEND KYOUKO HAS EVER BROUGHT OVER.
MAMI-SAN, I HOPE YOU AND KYOUKO WILL BE LONG-LASTING, GOOD FRIENDS.
AAAHH!
I TOLD YOU TO KEEP THAT SECRET!

MAMI-SAN, SORRY! I KEPT YOU OUT SO LATE!
BUT IF IT'S OKAY WITH YOU, COME OVER AGAIN!
YES......
HM?

SAKURA-SAN?
YOUR WISH AS A MAGICAL GIRL...

...YEAH.
IT'S JUST...
I WASN'T WISHING FOR US TO BECOME RICH OR ANYTHING.
...I WANTED ALL THE PEOPLE TO LISTEN TO WHAT MY FATHER HAD TO SAY.
...THAT'S ALL.

NOT ONE PERSON TRIED TO UNDERSTAND WHAT HE WAS SAYING! NOBODY'D EVEN LISTEN!
I GOT FRUS-TRATED!
SO MUCH, I COULDN'T STAND IT.
...I SEE.
IT WAS FOR YOUR FATHER'S SAKE.
I MADE A WISH FOR SOME-BODY ELSE'S SAKE...
IS THAT REALLY SO WEIRD?
NO.
IT'S SIMPLY THAT I THINK ...
...THAT A WISH FOR SOMEONE ELSE...
...THAT ALSO FULFILLS A WISH FOR YOURSELF TOO WOULD BE A VERY WONDERFUL THING.
OUR BATTLES PUT US IN GREAT DANGER, AND AS AN ASPECT OF IT, WE MUST SACRIFICE AT LEAST PART OF OUR LIVES.
I FEEL THAT ONE CAN WITHSTAND THE PRICE OF A WISH BETTER IF IT'S FOR ONESELF.
BUT IF IT ISN'T......

IF THAT'S THE CASE, THEN I'M ALL RIGHT.
I'VE BEEN WATCHING MY FATHER SINCE I WAS LITTLE...
...AND HE'S BEEN DOING EVERYTHING TO MAKE US HAPPY.
I WANTED HAPPINESS FOR EVERYONE, MYSELF INCLUDED.
AND THE FIRST STEP TO THAT...
...WAS TO MAKE SURE MY FATHER IS HAPPY.
YEP. THAT'S THE DEAL.

I'M HERE TO PROTECT EVERYBODY'S HAPPINESS!
THAT'S REALLY WHAT MY WISH IS!
OF COURSE...
I'M SURE YOU'LL BE JUST FINE.

THAT MAKES MY REASON FOR FIGHTING THE SAME AS YOURS, MAMI-SAN!
EH?
I'LL JUST SAY IT AGAIN! LET'S KEEP WORKING TOGETHER!
YES...

PO (POHH)
MY SOUL GEM JUST REACTED.
MAMI, KYOUKO?
I'VE FOUND A GRIEF SEED!
A WITCH IS TRYING TO HATCH FROM IT.
YOU'D BETTER HURRY.

I CANNOT HELP BUT THINK SHE IS DIFFERENT FROM OTHER MAGICAL GIRLS.

I NEVER THOUGHT TWO MAGICAL GIRLS COULD UNDERSTAND EACH OTHER SO WELL!

SAKURA-SAN, YOUR ATTACK IS CALLED "ROSSO FANTASMA!"
(IT MEANS, "RED GHOST.")
EVER SINCE I DECIDED...
...TO PROTECT THE PEOPLE AS A MAGICAL GIRL...
...SOMEWHERE INSIDE OF ME, I WANTED...
...THE PERFECT PARTNER.

AND FINALLY, I WAS ABLE TO MEET HER!
IF IT'S THE TWO OF US...
THERE ISN'T AN ENEMY THAT CAN STAND AGAINST THE COMBO OF MAMI-SAN AND ME!
JYAAAAAN (TAH-DAAAH)
...THEN EVEN WALPURGIS NACHT WOULD GO DOWN EASY!
HONESTLY...! WE MUSTN'T GET OVER-CONFIDENT!

WAL-PURGIS... IS THAT ...?
THAT'S THE ONE!
THAT HUGE WITCH THAT ALL THE MAGICAL GIRLS' RUMORS ARE ABOUT.
I MAY BE OVERCONFIDENT HERE, BUT...
...I DON'T THINK EVEN A BIG WITCH LIKE THAT COULD STAND UP TO US!
WE COULD EVEN SAVE THE WHOLE WORLD!
...IS WHAT I THINK!
I'M GETTING AHEAD OF MYSELF?
I WOULDN'T SAY THAT.
AND I THINK IT'S GOOD TO HAVE BIG GOALS.
...HEH-HEH-HEH...
YOU HAVE GOTTEN CONFIDENT, HAVEN'T YOU?
EH?
HEH HEH HEH HEH
MAMI-SAN, YOU'RE LAUGHING TOO MUCH!
...HOW-EVER... YOU MAY BE RIGHT.

I, TOO, THINK THAT THE TWO OF US COULD TAKE DOWN SUCH A WITCH.
AND IF SOMEDAY...
...WALPURGIS NACHT WERE TO ACTUALLY COME HERE...
...THEN LET'S PROTECT THE TOWN TOGETHER.
SHU (GLEAM)

MM...?
SUUUU

...!?
BASA
(SHIFT)
KYOUKO!

THIS
IS BAD.

WHAT
...
...IS THIS
SMELL?

GII
(KREEK)
KIIIIII
(KREEEEEEK)

BASA (FLIP)
WE NEVER NEEDED ANY "WORD OF GOD" TO START WITH!
WE KNOW A REALLY EASY WAY TO FIND CONTENT-MENT...
...WITHOUT RELYING ON THIS CRAP.
DOPUN (GLUG)
YEAH!
YOU'RE RIGHT ABOUT THAT!
WHA...
WHAT'S WITH...
...THESE GUYS ...!?
GO (VOOM)
GO
THEY'RE UNDER A WITCH'S CURSE.
THE WARDS ARE STARTING TO SPREAD.

TON
TON (TONK)
TO
SU (SST)
!
THEY INTEND TO BURN THE ENTIRE CHURCH!
I WILL NOT ALLOW THAT!
GYU (KLENCH)
KA (FLASH)

POHYUN (PO-FOOM)
BARA (CRUMBLE)
KOOO (HYUUU)
PASHIN (GRAB)
TAN (TMP)
TAN
THAT ONE'S MINE!

POHYU (PO-FOOM)
ZU
ZU
ZU
I HOPE YOU'RE PREPARED FOR THIS.
ZU (ZUMM)
KOOO (FWOOO)
IT'S MY FATHER'S CHURCH...
...THAT YOU CAST YOUR STINKING CURSE ON!
GO (FOOM)
AND YOU'RE GONNA PAY FOR IT!
PO (POHH)

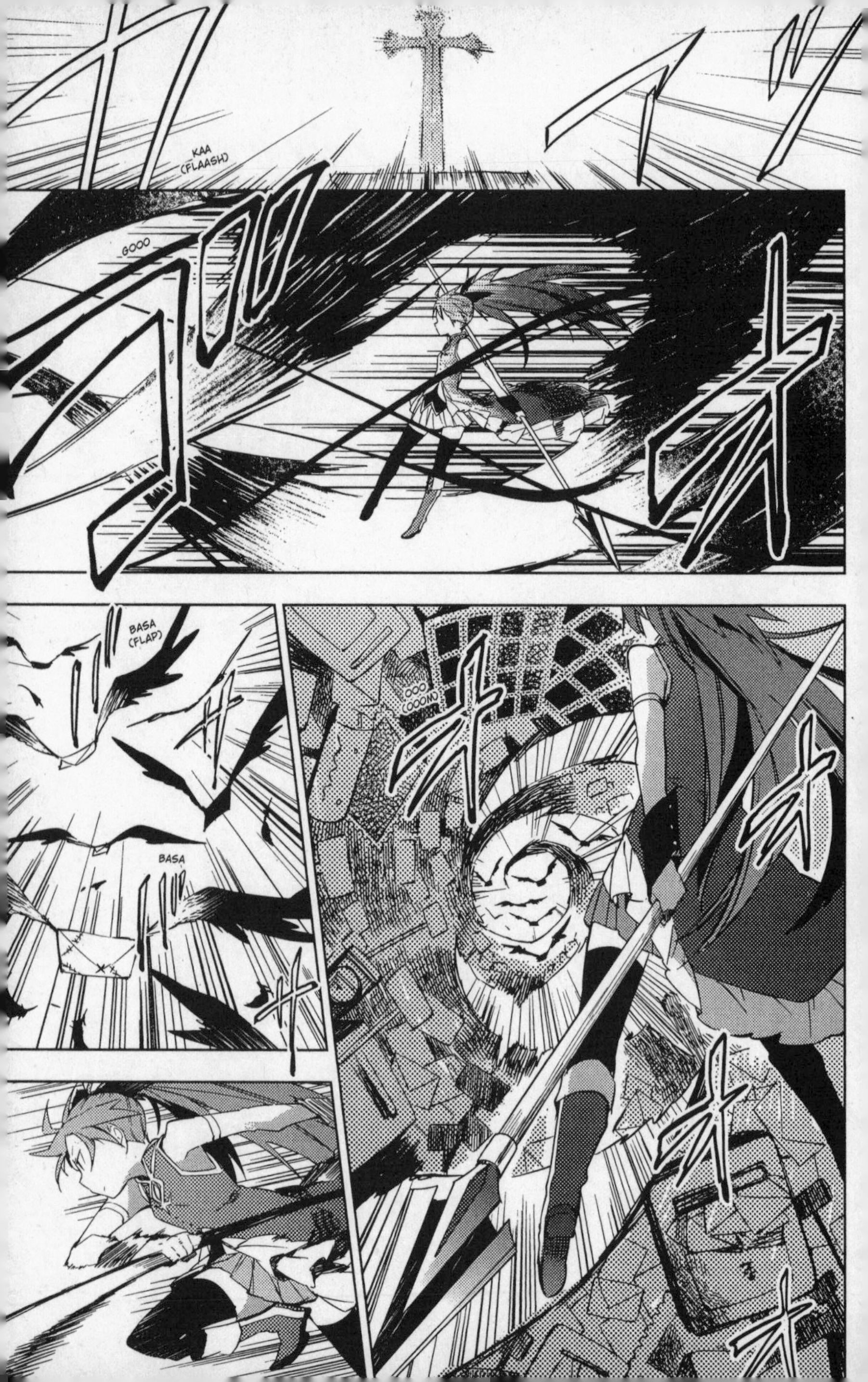
KAA
(FLAASH)
GOOO
BASA
(FLAP)
OOO
(OOOM)
BASA

BASASA
(FLAFF)
BYUO
(VYOOOM)
HUMPH!
OH, GOOD.
FUO
(FOOM)
I DON'T HAVE TO GO TO YOU SINCE YOU'RE COMING TO ME!

THAT'S A REAL TIME-SAVER!
ZASHU (ZLASH)
BUSHI (BLOOSH)
KYU (TWIRL)
GACHIN (KACHANK)

WHOOPS!
GUN (PULL)
GAKIN (KACHUNK)
HYUU (FOOM)
WHA ...!?
YOU LITTLE...
BASA (FLAP)
AH!
BASA
BASA

BASA
COME ON...
HYUOOOOO

GAN (KLANG)

YORO (WOBBLE)
KAN (TAK)
YOU'RE A PRETTY STUBBORN ONE, AIN'T YA?
ARE YOU THAT UPSET ABOUT NOT BEING ABLE TO EAT A FEW HUMANS?
SORRY, BUT...
...I'M NOT GONNA LET YOU EAT EVEN ONE OF THEM!
GO (WHOOM)

KASHI (SHING)
NO WITCH...
...IS GOING TO RUN WILD THROUGH THIS PLACE!
GU (PULL)
MY FATHER'S CHURCH...
FUON (FOOM)
MY FAMILY...
EVERY-BODY...
I'M GOING TO PROTECT ALL OF THEM!

HYU
(VOOM)
JAKIN
(ZLASSH)
GOOOOO
(WHOOHHH)

KIN
(CHINK)
SIGH
......!
TSUN
(SNIFF)
...THEY LEAVE BEHIND A HARD-TO-CLEAN MESS.
—BUT IT'S OKAY. THERE'S PLENTY OF TIME BEFORE DAWN...
KI
(KREEK)
THAT'S WHEN THIS WOULD ALL GET COMPLICATED...

......KYOUKO?

MOMO.
JUST LIKE KYOUKO, SINCE SHE'S A LITTLE MORE MATURE THAN IN THE ANIME, HER HAIR STYLE IS SLIGHTLY DIFFERENT.

PUELLA MAGI
MADOKA★MAGICA
~The different story~

KII
(KREEK)

KYOUKO...
WHERE ARE YOU...?

...DADDY?
WHERE'S KYOUKO?
WHAT'S WRONG?

MM...
SORRY FOR WAKING YOU.
?
IT'S NOTHING. GO BACK TO SLEEP.
GOOD NIGHT, MOMO.

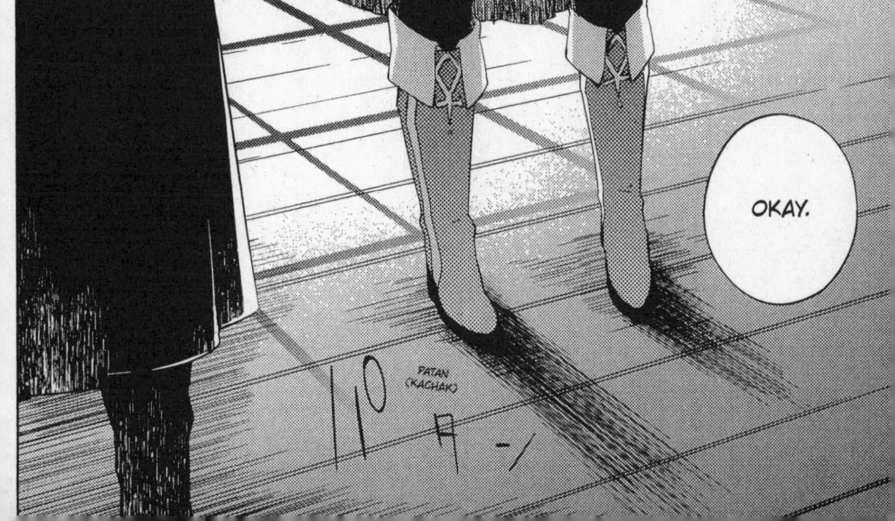
OKAY.
PATAN (KACHAK)

EPISODE 3

SAKURA-SAN, ARE YOU NOT FEELING WELL?
YOU'VE BEEN LOOKING A LITTLE PALE RECENTLY.

THINK SO?
I'M FINE.
REALLY?
......I GET THE FEELING SOMETHING HAPPENED TO YOU.
MAMI-SAN, HAVE YOU EVER...

...HAD ARGUMENTS WITH SOMEONE YOU WERE CLOSE TO BECAUSE YOU BECAME A MAGICAL GIRL?

DO YOU THINK THAT IT CAN WORK THE OPPOSITE WAY TOO?
JUST BECAUSE WE SAVE SOMEBODY WHO WAS CURSED...
...IT DOESN'T NECESSARILY MEAN THEY'RE GOING TO GET THEMSELVES A HAPPY ENDING.
...WHAT DO YOU MEAN?
FOR EXAMPLE...

...SAY SOMEBODY DRIVEN CRAZY BY A WITCH'S CURSE...
...TRIES TO COMMIT SUICIDE IN THEIR RAVINGS...
AND SAY ONE OF THEIR NEIGHBORS HAPPENS TO ACCIDENTALLY SEE IT, WHAT DO YOU THINK WOULD HAPPEN?

EVEN IF A MAGICAL GIRL COMES IN AND STOPS THEIR SUICIDE...
...WOULD THAT NEIGHBOR EVER LOOK AT THEM THE SAME WAY AGAIN?

OR WOULD THE NEIGHBOR ...
...ALWAYS LOOK SUSPICIOUSLY AT THE VICTIM...
...AND SAY, "THAT GUY'S JUST INSANE!"

AND IF...
...IT TURNS OUT TO NOT HAVE A HAPPY ENDING...
...THEN BETWEEN BEING KILLED BY A WITCH AND HAVING EVERYONE MOURN YOU LIKE NORMAL...
...OR CONTINUING TO LIVE WHILE HAVING SOMEBODY YOU LOVE AVOID YOU FOR THE REST OF YOUR LIFE.
...I WONDER WHICH IS BETTER.
IF IT'S JUST GONNA CAUSE PAIN FOR EVERYONE...
...WOULD IT BE BETTER NOT TO SAVE SOMEONE TO BEGIN WITH?
WHO ARE YOU TALKING ABOUT?
....
YOUR FAMILY WASN'T ATTACKED BY A WITCH, WERE THEY...?
NOTHING LIKE THAT.
IT'S JUST A HYPO-THETICAL STORY.
IT'S JUST...
...LIKE YOU WERE NEVER ABLE TO TALK TO ANYBODY ABOUT BEING A MAGICAL GIRL...
...IT'S HARD TO MAKE A NORMAL PERSON WHO'S NEVER HEARD OF WITCHES...
...GET ANY KIND OF CLUE AS TO WHAT IT IS WE GO THROUGH.

IT'S TRUE...
...WE CAN'T SAY WHAT WE DO...
...IS THE RIGHT THING IN ALL CIRCUMSTANCES FOR ALL PEOPLE.
STILL, IF WE DON'T DO WHAT WE DO, IT'LL RESULT IN EVEN MORE SACRIFICES.
AND I CAN'T SAY THAT I AGREE...
...THAT WE SHOULD NOT SAVE PEOPLE USING THE EXCUSE THAT WE DON'T KNOW THE END RESULT.
....
JUST MAKE SURE YOU DON'T PUSH YOURSELF TOO HARD.
AND IF YOU DON'T MIND CONFIDING IN ME, I'LL BE HERE TO LISTEN.
...... OKAY...

...I'M HOME.

THERE ARE MORE...
...LIQUOR BOTTLES...
YOU'LL RUIN YOUR HEALTH.

......
LISTEN...
...DAD...
I WENT OUT AND DEFEATED A WITCH TODAY TOO.
I SAVED THIS GUY WHO WAS ABOUT TO COMMIT SUICIDE.

THOSE SEEDS OF DISCONTENT AND SADNESS THAT YOU WANT SO MUCH TO BANISH...
WE'RE GOING OUT AS MAGICAL GIRLS AND REMOVING THE SOURCE!

THAT CAN'T BE A BAD THING, RIGHT?

I ALWAYS LOVED YOUR SERMONS. I STILL DO!
SO I WAS SO HAPPY WHEN PEOPLE STARTED LISTENING TO YOU!
WHAT MADE ME HAPPIEST...
...WAS SEEING YOUR HAPPY FACE...
...EVEN AMID ALL THE DISCONTENT AND SADNESS IN THE WORLD.
YOU SEE, FOR ME...
IT'S ALL JUST AN ILLUSION THAT YOU MADE, ISN'T IT?
ALL THOSE PEOPLE WHO CAME TO HEAR ME WASN'T BECAUSE THEY BELIEVED...
...BUT BECAUSE A WITCH USED HER POWER TO ENTRANCE THEM. THAT'S ALL.
THOSE POOR PEOPLE.
AND YOU WERE GOING TO KILL THOSE POOR, CONFUSED PEOPLE, CORRECT?
IT WAS ALL A RESULT THAT CAME FROM YOUR UNGODLY CONTRACT WITH THE DEVIL, WASN'T IT?
A DAUGHTER OF A CHURCH SOLD HER SOUL TO THE DEVIL...
......!

LIKE I'VE BEEN SAYING...I'VE TOLD YOU THIS OVER AND OVER! WITCHES AND MAGICAL GIRLS ARE COMPLETELY DIFFERENT!
I'M BEGGING YOU, JUST TRUST ME IN THIS!
I WOULD NEVER TAKE ANYBODY'S LIFE!!
I'M NOT A WITCH...
...FROM THE VERY START, YOU THOUGHT...

...THAT YOU SHOULDN'T LISTEN TO A WORD I SAY...
...MY WORDS ARE SIMPLY NONSENSE THAT COULDN'T SAVE ANYONE.
ISN'T THAT TRUE?

YES, AND YOU'D BE CORRECT. I HAVE NO POWER TO SAVE THE LOST SOULS OF THIS WORLD.
AND I GAVE THE DEVIL THE OPENING NEEDED TO LEAD THEM TO DESTRUC-TION!
IT ISN'T YOUR FAULT. I MUST TAKE RESPONSIBILITY FOR IT ALL.
...WHAT ARE YOU SAYING...
THAT'S NOT IT.
DAD... YOU'RE WRONG...

"WRONG"? WHAT IS?
TELLING ME THAT WITH YOUR POWER...
...YOU'VE BEEN DEFEATING THE SEEDS OF SADNESS AND MISERY OF THE WORLD...
RATHER THAN LISTENING TO NONSENSE EXCUSES LIKE THAT...
...I'D RATHER BE CALLED AN IMPOTENT LOSER!

JUST WHAT DO YOU THINK YOU'RE DOING RIGHT NOW?
SAYING THE WORLD CAN SAVE ITSELF WITHOUT ME...
...THAT'S THE DEVIL'S TALK AS HE GRINDS BELIEVERS UNDER HIS HEEL AND LAUGHS AT THEIR PAIN, IS IT NOT?
AND YOU, HAPPILY REPEATING THE DEVIL'S WORDS AND NEVER REALIZING IT...
IF I CAN'T CALL YOU A WITCH, WHAT CAN I CALL YOU?

KII
(CREAK)
...!!
...!
...!?

GIN (CLANG)
TIRO...
...FINALE!
DOO (DOOM)

SAKURA-SAN...
...DIDN'T COME TODAY EITHER, HMM?
...SHE'S ALL RIGHT, ISN'T SHE?
SAKURA-SAN ISN'T LIKE THE OTHERS.
HOW...CAN YOU STILL NOT UNDERSTAND?
IT ISN'T JUST THE WITCHES WHO ATTACK PEOPLE! THE FAMILIARS—
WRONG. HOLD IT A SECOND.
IT'S TIME FOR YOU TO HEAR ME OUT!

IF WE DO WHAT YOU'RE TELLING US TO DO...
...THEN WE MIGHT RUN OUT OF GRIEF SEEDS COMPLETELY!
AND IT'LL BE ALL YOUR FAULT, RIGHT?
IT'S ALL BECAUSE FAMILIARS GROW UP THAT WE HAVE WITCHES AT ALL!
SO I THINK WE HAVE TO TURN OUR BACKS AND LET THE FAMILIARS HAVE A SACRIFICE OR TWO.
IT ISN'T LIKE IT'S EASY TO FIND WITCHES, RIGHT?
I THINK IT'S A GOOD THING! THAT AMBITION OF YOURS...
...TO WANT TO SAVE EVERY HUMAN YOU CAN...
...BUT...
...KYUBEY...
IS WHAT I'M TRYING TO DO SO ODD?
I CAN'T SAY ONE WAY OR THE OTHER.
HOWEVER, I CAN SAY THAT YOUR TYPE IS LESS COMMON.
...I SEE.
BUT DON'T LET IT GET YOU DOWN.
IT'S THE PATH YOU DECIDED ON, RIGHT?

MAMI-SAN...

MAMI-SAN, YOU'RE MY IDEAL IN EVERY WAY.

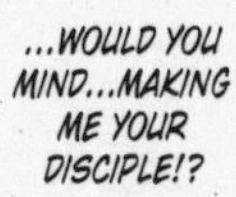
...WOULD YOU MIND...MAKING ME YOUR DISCIPLE!?

WHAT'S WRONG?

...IT'S NOTHING.
LET'S GO HOME.
HOW ABOUT DINNER? IS THERE ANYTHING YOU'RE HUNGRY FOR?

I WONDER WHAT'S HAPPENED TO SAKURA-SAN.

I DON'T KNOW IF I CAN MAKE IT ANY BETTER, BUT...
WE NEED TO TAKE A BREAK FROM OUR CONSTANT BATTLES TO REFRESH OURSELVES.
MAYBE WE COULD GO FOR CAKES OR COOK SOMETHING TOGETHER...
...MAYBE THERE IS SOMETHING I CAN DO.
KUSHUN (ACHOO)
...IT'S GOTTEN COLD RECENTLY.
MAYBE WE COULD EAT SOME WARM FOOD TOGETHER.

THAT MAKES MY REASON FOR FIGHTING...
...THE SAME AS YOURS, MAMI-SAN!
IF IT'S THE TWO OF US THEN EVEN WALPURGIS NACHT WOULD GO DOWN EASY!
...THEN LET'S PROTECT THE TOWN TOGETHER.
......KYUBEY...
DO YOU KNOW ABOUT SAKURA-SAN...
?

......NEVER MIND.
I HAVE TO GIVE IT MY BEST AGAIN TODAY!
EVEN IF I DO IT ALONE.

I HAVE TO...
...PROTECT THIS TOWN!

And next, we bring you the news.
Last night, just before dawn, a fire broke out...
...in the town of Kazamino. Neighbors of the residence were able to call it in.
The firefighters on the scene reported that the fire was quickly extinguished...
...however, a portion of the building was burned to the ground.
The firefighters recovered three bodies, presumed to be residents of the house.

The victims were identified as members of the...
...Sakura family...

...a report from the scene.
The police state that there is a high probability of this being a murder-suicide case. However they continue to investigate.
SAKURA... SAN?

KYOUKO?
AREN'T YOU GOING OUT TO FIGHT WITCHES?
YOU HAVEN'T PURIFIED YOUR SOUL GEM IN QUITE A WHILE.
YOU HAVE TO DEFEAT A WITCH AND GET YOUR HANDS ON A GRIEF SEED.
OR YOU WON'T BE ABLE TO FIGHT ANYMORE.

I DON'T NEED THE POWER ANYMORE.

I WAS A FOOL TO TRUST IN THE POWER OF A MIRACLE RIGHT FROM THE START.

IF A POWER LIKE THIS CAN'T HELP ME PROTECT WHAT'S REALLY IMPORTANT TO ME...

KYUBEY...
IF I WERE TO JUST STOP HUNTING WITCHES...
...COULD I DIE JUST LIKE EVERYBODY ELSE?

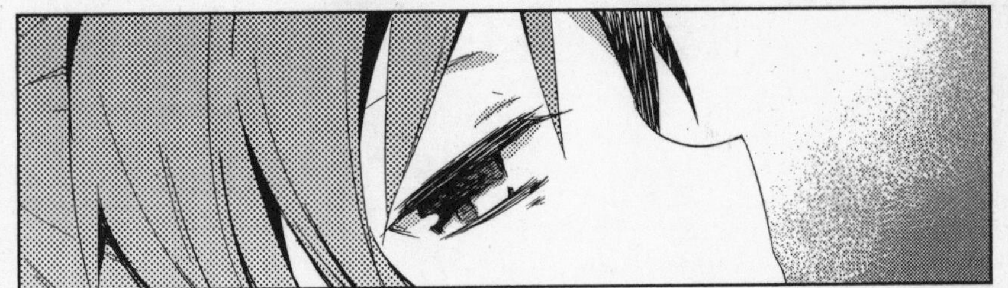

I'M JUST KIDDING. YOU KNOW THAT.

GYARI
(KLANG)
GI
GI
(GRIND)
GI
GI
KYURURURU
(VLUUM)

DO
(BOOM)
DO
DO
DO
GOO
(RUMBLE)
BUO
(VWOO)
TAN
(TUMP)
HYU
(FOOM)
HYUN

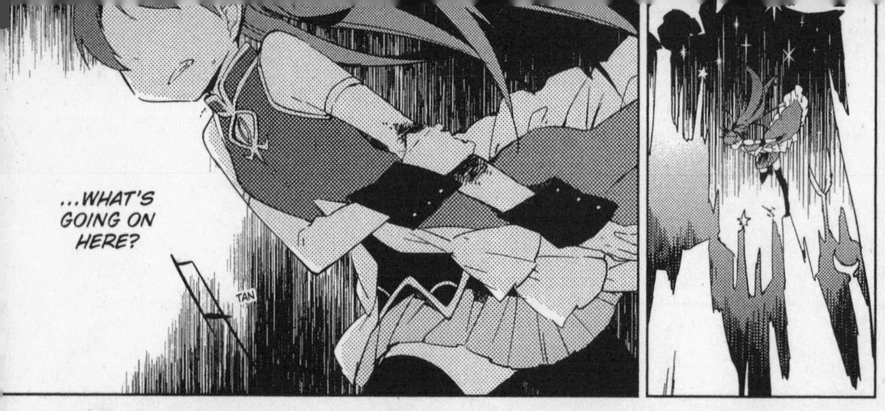

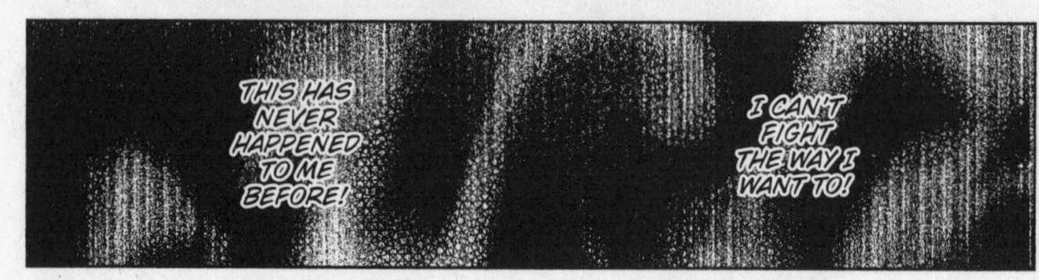

WHY CAN'T I REMEMBER...

...HOW TO DO MAGIC RIGHT?

GU..
...UHH...
ZU (ZLUSH)
KYURURU (VLUUM)
ZAA (SLASH)
KAN (KLANG)
...!
FUU (WHOOSH)

GA
(KRACK)
GAAH!
HYUN
(FYOOM)
ZA
(ZLISH)
GARAN
(CLANG)
DO
(WHUD)
PAKI
(PACHIK)
URG...
PAKI—
PAKI
PAKI

PAKI
(PACHIK)
PAKI
PAKI
PAKI
I HEAR EVEN THE MAIN CHURCH OF HIS RELIGION...
...HAS EXCOMMUNI-CATED HIM.

YEAH... I HEAR HE WAS GIVING SOME STRANGE SERMONS LATELY...
IT'S JUST ANOTHER CULT CAUSING PROBLEMS!
BEST TO NOT GET INVOLVED.
KYOUKO, I'M HUNGRY!
IT'LL BE ALL RIGHT, MOMO.
THEY'LL COME AROUND TO UNDERSTANDING WHAT DAD IS TRYING TO SAY!
THEN WE'LL BE ABLE TO EAT UNTIL WE'RE FULL!
BUT UNTIL THEN, WE JUST HAVE TO HOLD OUT.
HAVE AN APPLE.
EH-HEH-HEH! I GOT IT ON THE SLY.
DID YOU? SOMEONE GAVE YOU THIS?
I'LL JUST GO CUT IT FOR YOU.

HERE! THIS IS YOUR PORTION, KYOUKO.
?
BUT THAT'S ALL OF IT.
SPLIT IT UP AMONG EVERYBODY.
I CAN'T EAT IT ALL MYSELF!
THIS IS HOW IT SHOULD BE. IT WAS A PRESENT TO YOU.
WE HAVE NO NEED OF IT.
DAD, WELCOME HOME!
SHALL WE BE OFF, HONEY? MOMO?
YEAH!
YES.
...... OFF TO WHERE?

SAY, DAD? MOM? MOMO?
DON'T LEAVE ME HERE ALONE!
WHERE ARE YOU ALL GOING?
...WHERE? YOU KNOW WHERE.
ZAAAA (SHHHHH)

GYUU (GRIP)
KAA (FLASH)
DOSHU (GUSH)

PIKU (TWITCH)
GAKUN (SLUMP)
WHEEZE
NOW THAT COULD CAUSE PROBLEMS.
PANT
JUUUU (ZLUUSSH)
KYOUKO.
YOU CAN'T USE YOUR MAGIC ANYMORE, RIGHT?
.... WHY NOT?

BECAUSE YOU SAID YOU DIDN'T NEED IT.
....

THE POWER THAT WAS BORN FROM YOUR WISH WAS "FASCINATION."
AND SUBCONSCIOUSLY, YOU REJECTED YOUR OWN WISH.
THE ATTRIBUTES OF THE MAGIC THAT ANY MAGICAL GIRL IS GIVEN...
...ARE DIRECTLY CONNECTED TO THE WISH THAT GIRL MAKES.

IF YOUR POWERS DON'T COME BACK...
...YOU'LL BE AT AN ENORMOUS HANDICAP IN ANY FUTURE BATTLES.

......HA-HA...
IS THAT RIGHT?

SO IT'S ALL MY OWN DAMN FAULT.

I REALLY CAN'T BE SAVED...
THE WHOLE REASON I BECAME A MAGICAL GIRL...
...WAS TO PROTECT FATHER AND MY FAMILY...
...AND THIS IS HOW IT TURNED OUT.
NOW I CAN'T...
...EVEN PROTECT MYSELF LIKE I WANT.
PAKIN (CRACKL)

SAKU
(SHK)

MAMI-SA...
YOU'RE SO COLD!
YOU'RE EVEN SHIVERING!
PLUS, YOU'RE BADLY WOUNDED!
A WITCH DID THIS TO YOU?
I'LL MAKE YOU BETTER, SO JUST STAY STILL.
......

BUT I'M SO GLAD TO FIND YOU!
I HADN'T SEEN YOU IN FOREVER.
YOU HAD ME WORRIED!

...I'M SORRY MAMI-SAN...
...BUT I DON'T THINK WE CAN DO THIS ANYMORE—
I'M SORRY!
I'LL BET IT WAS SO HARD ON YOU ALL ALONE...
I GUESS I FAIL AS A SENPAI.
I SHOULD HAVE GONE TO BE WITH YOU MUCH SOONER! I KNOW THAT NOW!
BUT I'M SO HAPPY THAT YOU'RE STILL ALIVE!

......
SNIFF...
...!

......IT'S ALL...
ALL OF IT IS MY FAULT!
I'M THE REASON...

PUELLA MAGI
MADOKA★MAGICA
~The different story~

HERE YOU GO.
I MADE YOU GINGER TEA.
EPISODE 4
I THOUGHT IT MIGHT HELP WARM YOU UP.
THANK YOU.
YOU EVEN LOANED ME CLOTHES...
I'M REALLY PUTTING YOU OUT, HUH?
NO PROBLEM.
IT'S LATE ALREADY. YOU SHOULD JUST STAY OVER.

...SAY...
...SAKURA-SAN...
WHAT ARE YOU THINKING OF DOING NOW?

I'M SURE YOU DON'T NEED TO HEAR...
...ANY SUGGESTIONS FROM ME, BUT...
...IF IT'S ALL RIGHT WITH YOU, YOU COULD STAY WITH ME UNTIL THINGS SETTLE DOWN FOR YOU AGAIN...

NO...

I REALLY APPRECIATE THE OFFER, BUT I THINK I'LL PASS.
I CAN'T IMPOSE ON YOU THAT MUCH.

...I SEE. IF YOU'VE GOT SOMEPLACE TO BE, THEN THAT'S FINE, BUT...
....

STOP TRYING TO DO EVERYTHING ON YOUR OWN.
I CAN PROVIDE BACKUP IN BATTLES TOO.
SO LET'S DO THINGS TOGETHER FROM NOW ON TOO, OKAY?
IT'S A LITTLE LATE, BUT I'LL FIX US UP SOMETHING SIMPLE FOR DINNER.
...OKAY.
PATAN (KACHIK)
SORRY, MAMI-SAN...
...BUT I'M AFRAID...
...I CAN'T FIGHT WITH YOU ANYMORE.

YOU'RE STILL NOT YOUR USUAL SELF.
THIS MAY BE HARD FOR YOU TO HEAR RIGHT NOW, BUT...
...IF YOU CAN'T GIVE IT EVERYTHING YOU GOT, YOU'D BETTER NOT FIGHT AT ALL.
YOUR LIFE IS RIDING ON IT, AFTER ALL.

WHAT YOU JUST FOUGHT BACK THERE WAS A FAMILIAR, SO YOU CAME AWAY WITH JUST A FEW WOUNDS...
...BUT IF YOU HAD YOUR FASCINATION MAGIC...
...YOU WOULDN'T HAVE EVEN TAKEN A SCRATCH.
WHY AREN'T YOU USING IT?
...I CAN TAKE DOWN A WITCH WITHOUT IT.
...?
WAIT A SECOND, SAKURA-SAN...
IT ISN'T LIKE JUST DEFEATING WITCHES IS...
OH, YEAH. NOW THAT I'VE GOT YOU HERE...
THERE'S SOME-THING...
...I'VE BEEN MEANING TO TALK TO YOU ABOUT.

IT'S ABOUT HOW WE FIGHT.
FROM NOW ON...
...INSTEAD OF TAKING DOWN THE WITCH AND ALL THE FAMILIARS...
...WHY DON'T WE JUST CONCENTRATE ON THE WITCH?

IF WE'RE HUNTING FAMILIARS EVEN THOUGH THEY DON'T DROP GRIEF SEEDS...
...THEN IT MEANS WE'RE WASTING OUR MAGIC FOR NO GOOD REASON.

HAS SOMETHING HAPPENED, SAKURA-SA—
YOU MAY BE TRYING TO BE A HERO AND "PROTECT THE PEACE" OR SOMETHING...
...BUT TO TELL YOU THE TRUTH, IT'S TOO MUCH OF A PAIN TO PLAY ALONG WITH YOUR HOBBIES ANYMORE.

WE DON'T PROFIT FROM THE SMALL FRIES, SO IT'S JUST A WASTE GOING AFTER THEM, RIGHT?

I GUESS IT JUST DOESN'T SEEM RIGHT TO ME ANYMORE...
...WHAT ARE YOU TALKING ABOUT...?

IT COULD BE A WITCH OR A FAMILIAR, BUT IF THEY GET LOOSE, PEOPLE ARE GOING TO DIE!
SO WE HAVE TO—
THAT'S WHY I'M SAYING...
...WE CAN'T GO SAVING EVERYBODY ALL THE TIME, RIGHT!?
....
WHY DO I HAVE TO RISK MY LIFE TO SAVE JERKS LIKE THAT!?
WHETHER THEY'RE POSSESSED BY A WITCH OR NOT...
...THE ONES WHO WANT TO DIE ARE GONNA DIE!
I SAY LET THE FAMILIARS EAT 'EM!
JUST AS LONG AS THEY BECOME A WAY FOR US TO GET GRIEF SEEDS!
... SAKURA-SAN...
...I UNDERSTAND HOW YOU FEEL ABOUT YOUR FAMILY, BUT...
...YOU STILL SHOULDN'T SAY—
YEAH? WHAT DO YOU UNDERSTAND?

A GIRL WHOSE FAMILY DIED IN AN ACCI-DENT...
...IS IN NO WAY THE SAME AS A GIRL WHOSE FAMILY DIED BECAUSE OF HER, RIGHT?
BUT HEY, YOU WERE RIGHT ABOUT ONE THING.
I REALLY SHOULD HAVE MADE THE WISH FOR MYSELF.
IF I DID, THE ONLY ONE HURT WOULD BE ME.
THAT WAY, YOU DON'T PUSH YOUR OWN SELFISH IDEAS OF HAPPINESS ON SOMEBODY ELSE!
HERE I GOT MY WHOLE FAMILY CAUGHT UP IN MY OWN MISERY...
SERVES ME RIGHT! AFTER ALL, IT WAS MY MAGIC THAT STARTED THE WHOLE TRAIN WRECK!
I'LL BET SOMEWHERE DOWN INSIDE...
...YOU THOUGHT SOMETHING LIKE THIS WAS BOUND TO HAPPEN, RIGHT...?
I... NEVER...

SO I MADE UP MY MIND.
I'M NOT GOING TO DO ANYTHING MORE FOR OTHER PEOPLE'S HAPPINESS.
OR TRY TO SAVE ANYBODY ANYMORE.
I'LL NEVER USE MY MAGIC FOR THAT REASON!
I'M ONLY EVER GOING TO USE MY MAGIC TO MAKE ME HAPPY!
...SO WE'RE DONE HERE, RIGHT?
YOU DESPISE ME NOW, DON'T YOU?
WE CAN'T FIGHT TOGETHER ANYMORE, HUH?
YOU AND ME END RIGHT HERE...

!?
......I...
LET ME GO!
...NO, I CAN'T!
I DON'T CARE HOW TOUGH IT IS FOR YOU RIGHT NOW...
...I CAN'T LET YOU CHOOSE A LIFE LIKE THAT!
HERE YOU GO, TRYING TOO HARD TO ACT STRONG...
...EVEN THOUGH IT'S GOING TO MAKE THINGS EVEN TOUGHER FOR YOU!
HOW CAN I LEAVE YOU ALONE LIKE THIS!?

I CAN'T JUST WALK AWAY FROM YOU LIKE THIS!
I JUST CAN'T.
OKAY, THEN...
KMA!
GOO (VWOOH)
I'M LEAVING IF I HAVE TO BLAST YOU AWAY TO DO IT!

TAN (TUMP)
ZA (SHIK)
......I SEE.
YOU DON'T INTEND TO TALK THIS OVER RATIONALLY, CORRECT?
BUA (VWAAH)
YOU REALLY...
...ARE ALWAYS CAUSING YOUR SENPAI PROBLEMS!

DA (DASH)
SORRY...
...SENPAI!
DOGA (BAKOOM)

KYUUU
(KOOOOM)
BUT I CAN SEE RIGHT THROUGH IT, NO PROBLEM!
HYU
(FOOM)
YOU GOT HIGH-SPEED MAGIC!

...YOU MAY SAY THAT...
GIII (KEEEN)
ATTACKING FROM THE FRONT WITHOUT PLANNING AHEAD...
HERE I WARNED YOU, OVER AND OVER, BUT YOU STILL DO IT, HMM?
チッ
CHI (CHICK)
DON (BLAM)
DO

BON
(POFF)
HYU
(FOOM)
DO
(BLAM)
BOFU
(BOFF)
A SMOKE
SCREEN...?

CHUIN
(CHANK)

DO (BLAM)
DO
DO
DO
HA!
WHAT ARE YOU AIMING AT?
THAT'S WHY I'M TELLING YOU YOU'RE TOO SOFT!
AND IF YOU DON'T SHOOT LIKE YOU REALLY MEAN TO KILL ME...
GAN (GANCH)
...IT MEANS I DON'T EVEN HAVE TO DODGE IT!
GOO (VWOOSH)

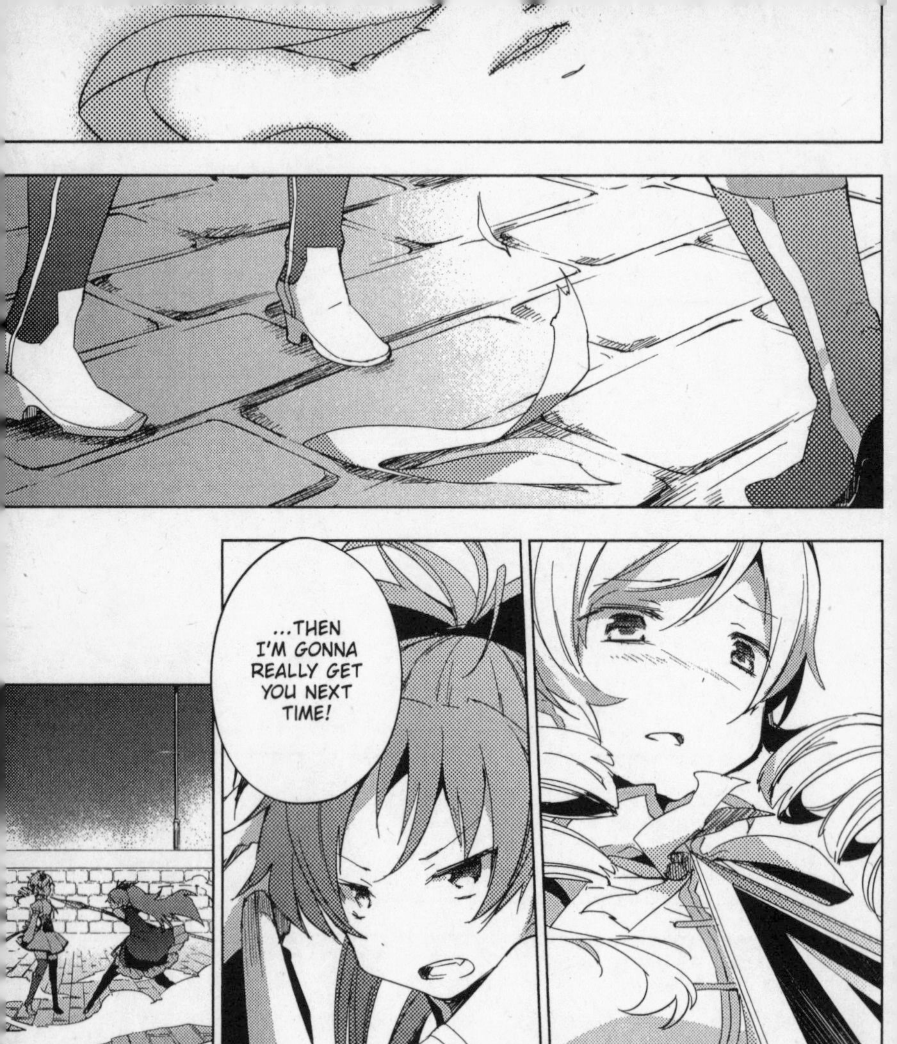

IF THIS CONTINUES...
...THEN I'M GONNA REALLY GET YOU NEXT TIME!
'COS UNLIKE YOU, I'M SERIOUS!

KAN (CLANG)
I'M GOING BACK TO KAZA-MINO.
FROM NOW ON, I'M GOING TO FIGHT MY WAY.
THANKS FOR THE LESSONS TILL NOW.
SAKURA-SAN...

YOU WERE...
...THE FIRST MAGICAL GIRL WHO EVER SAW EYE-TO-EYE WITH ME.

I BELIEVED YOU WEREN'T LIKE ALL THE OTHER MAGICAL GIRLS.

ARE YOU SURE THIS IS WHAT YOU WANT?

YOU REALLY THINK YOU CAN STAND THE LONELINESS?

...ANOTHER FAILURE.
WHY DOES IT ALWAYS...
...TURN OUT THIS WAY?
I'M BACK TO BEING ALL ALONE AGAIN.

YOU CAN FIND BETTER FRIENDS THAN ME.

—...

—SAN?

MAMI-SAN!
KIIIIIN CKEEEND

KANAME-SAN?
I'M SORRY. I DIDN'T REALIZE IT WAS YOU.
WHAT'S THE MATTER?
UM...
I'M SORRY! HERE I GO, CALLING ON YOU ALL OF A SUDDEN!
UH...
THIS ISN'T GOOD!

SAYAKA-CHAN IS...!
GA (KRACK)
KIN (CHANG)
KEEE (SHIING)
...HM?

HYU
(FOOM)
YOU'RE NOT TOO BAD FOR A ROOKIE.
LEARNED A LOT FROM THIS "SENPAI" YOU'VE BEEN BRAGGING ABOUT?
TO
(TUMP)
HMPH... YOU'RE NOTHING LIKE MAMI-SAN!
ONLY IN IT FOR YOURSELF!
AND YOU DON'T GIVE A DAMN ABOUT THE LIVES OF OTHER PEOPLE!
TA
(JUMP)
AIN'T NO WAY...

...I'M GONNA LET A MAGICAL GIRL LIKE YOU BEAT ME!
...HAH!
HYUA (FWOOM)
JARIN (CHANKLE)
YOU DON'T GET IT, DO YOU!?

GU (PULL)
FIGHTING FOR OTHER PEOPLE...
KA (CRACK)
... WON'T DO YOU ANY GOOD!
HYU
KA (CHANK)
BUT IF YOU'RE SUCH A FOOL YOU CAN'T FIGURE THAT OUT...
...THEN I GUESS I JUST GOTTA BEAT SOME SENSE INTO YOU!
KOTSUN (CLANK)

ZAA
(FWOO)
AH...
IT'S BEEN A WHILE.
WE MADE IT...!
I AM THAT GIRL'S SENPAI. I'M RESPONSIBLE FOR HER.
I WISH YOU WOULDN'T INVOLVE HER IN ANYTHING UNTOWARD.

SAKURA-SAN.
CHA (CHICK)
ISN'T IT SIMPLY AN ACT OF BAD MANNERS...
...TO GO SETTING FOOT IN SOMEONE ELSE'S TERRITORY?
...I DIDN'T EXPECT YOU.
I THOUGHT FOR SURE YOU'D HAVE ROTTED AWAY LONG AGO...
...MAMI-SENPAI.
To be continued...

THANK YOU SO MUCH FOR READING THIS FAR IN THE FIRST VOLUME OF THE SPIN-OFF MANGA. I NEVER EXPECTED THAT MAMI AND KYOUKO'S STORY WOULD TAKE AN ENTIRE BOOK! BUT I WOULD CONSIDER IT AN HONOR IF WE COULD MEET UP AGAIN IN THE NEXT VOLUME.

THIS WORK IS A BRAND-NEW SPIN-OFF
BASED ON THE ORIGINAL STORY.

PUELLA MAGI MADOKA☆MAGICA 1 ~The Different Story~

MAGICA QUARTET
HANOKAGE

Translation: William Flanagan • Lettering: Lys Blakeslee

Yen Press
Hachette Book Group
237 Park Avenue, New York, NY 10017

www.HachetteBookGroup.com
www.YenPress.com

Yen Press is an imprint of Hachette Book Group, Inc. The Yen Press name and logo are trademarks of Hachette Book Group, Inc.

First Yen Press Edition: March 2014

ISBN: 978-0-316-37051-6

10 9 8 7 6 5 4 3 2

BVG

Printed in the United States of America